The

Answers

Book for Kids!

Volume 5

20 Questions from Kids on Space and Astronomy

KEN HAM &
BODIE HODGE

Fourth Printing: December 2016

Master Books®
P.O. Box 726
Green Forest, AR 72638

Master Books® is a division of the New Leaf Publishing Group, Inc.

Printed in China

Book design by Terry White

ISBN 13: 978-0-89051-782-6
Library of Congress Control Number: 2008904921

All Scripture references are New King James Version unless otherwise noted.

Please visit our website for other great titles: www.masterbooks.com

Special thanks to the kids who contributed from around the world, as well as th kids from Cornerstone Classical Christian Academy for their submissions!

When you see this icon, there will be related Scripture references noted for parents to use in answering their children's, and even their own, questions.

Dear Kids,

We hope this book will help answer some of your questions about space and astronomy. We pray that you understand that the Bible is true and that it explains the universe that we live in.

We see many sad things happening in our world. And we all do bad things, too. This is because of sin. Because Adam, our mutual grandfather (about 6,000 years ago), sinned against God and ruined the perfect world God originally created, we suffer and die due to sin, too.

But God provided a means to save us from sin and death. He sent His Son Jesus into the world to become a man and die on our behalf. Christ died on the Cross, but He also rose again (came back to life). If we repent (feel sorry and turn from our sin) and believe in Jesus Christ as our Lord and Savior and in His Resurrection, we too will be saved and get to spend all eternity with God in heaven with all of His goodness. Please read these Scriptures in the order given:

Genesis 1:1, 1:31, 3:17–19; Romans 5:12, 3:23, 6:23, 10:9, 5:1

God bless you.

Ken and Bodie

3

Question: What day were the planets created?

Kyle

Age 6

Answer:

God set them in the firmament of the heavens to give light on the earth (Genesis 1:17).

According to God's Word, bodies out in space, like the sun, moon, and stars, were created on day 4 of the creation week. This is found in Genesis 1:14–19.

God called the sun, the greater light — and it dominates the day. God called the moon, the lesser light — and it dominates the night. Genesis 1:16 says, "He [God] made the stars also." The word that we translate "stars" also includes planets, comets, asteroids, and so on.

Many people incorrectly guess that the solar system and the planets formed from a spinning and collapsing nebula (a cloud of gas and dust) with the sun at the center and the planets, asteroids, and so on at various distances. This has never been observed or repeated; it is just a story to try to explain the universe without God.

God, who knows all things and who was there at the beginning, revealed in His Word that He was responsible for creating the sun, moon, and stars (including the planets). Be careful about the stories that man tells, especially when they disagree with God's Word. "It is better to trust in the LORD than to put confidence in man" (Psalm 118:8).

Romans 11:36

Question: What is the purpose of stars?

Paige

Age 9

Answer:

The stars actually have several purposes besides the obvious signs and seasons (Genesis 1:14). Here are a few others:

To give light: There are a number of purposes for the stars. One purpose was to give light on the earth (Genesis 1:17). They don't give much light to the earth, like the sun or even the moon does (by reflecting the sun's light to earth), but they do give *enough*. On a dark and clear night, when the moon is not out (called a "new moon"), ask your parents to go outside with you so you can see how much light the stars give on the earth.

For comparison: Another purpose for the stars is comparison. If you look up at the night sky, there are many stars. If you used a telescope, you'd almost see more stars than you could imagine! In Genesis 15:5, God told Abraham to look to the sky and number the stars, if he was able to. Then God said to Abraham that his offspring would be just as numerous as the stars! Wow!

To declare the glory of God: According to the Psalms, the heavens and God's handiwork in them declare the glory of God. At the Creation Museum, we have several planetarium shows, and one takes a look at the size of the universe. It is immense with stars and galaxies (massive clusters of stars). When our guests leave that show after viewing the heavens — the stars, nebulae, and everything else — they usually give the glory to God!

Genesis 1:17; Psalm 136:9; Genesis 15:5;
Deuteronomy 10:22; Psalm 19:1

HOLY
BIBLE

Question:

Where are the "waters" that are "above" the expanse? Is there water at the edge of the universe?

Sean

Age 11

Answer:

Thus God made the firmament, and divided the waters which were under the firmament from the waters which were above the firmament; and it was so (Genesis 1:7).

God created water on day 1 of the creation week. On the second day of creation, God separated the waters by placing an expanse or firmament between these waters. God basically took the water and made some go up and some go down, so that the waters were above and below. Then the waters below were gathered into one place and God called them "seas" on day 3. God called this expanse *between* the waters "heaven," though sometimes this is translated as "sky."

It is basically what is *above* the earth. This would include our atmosphere (inner space) and outer space. It's what you see when you stand outside and look up. There is no doubt that the first clouds (which are droplets of water, not vapor) were made during this expanse. The expanse extends far into space, though we don't know how far it really was. God made the sun, moon, and stars *in* the expanse on day 4 (Genesis 1:17). The universe would have to be really big in order to hold all the stars that are out there.

Genesis 1:6–8, 1:17

Question: Where does a week come from?

Caleb

Age 6

Answer:

For in six days the LORD made the heavens and the earth, the sea, and all that is in them, and rested the seventh day. Therefore the LORD blessed the Sabbath day and hallowed it (Exodus 20:11).

This question is very important! Let's look at some *other* time references (days, months, and years) first. A day is one rotation of the earth on its axis. A month ultimately comes from one revolution of the moon around the earth. A year comes from one revolution of the earth around the sun. A week (7 days) has nothing to do with *any* astronomical time reference. So where does a week come from? A week comes from the Bible, because God created in 6 days and He rested on the seventh day.

God, being God, didn't need to rest. He did that for our benefit. In Exodus 20:11, God explains that He created in 6 days and rested for one day as a basis for our workweek. This is why everyone works according to this pattern. Moses and the Israelites worked for 6 days and then rested on the seventh day (called the "Sabbath"). Exodus 31:17 is another confirmation that God created in six normal days and not over the millions and billions of years taught in the secular media and education system. God's Word can be trusted over any of these false myths that the earth is millions of years old.

Exodus 20:11, 31:17; 1 Timothy 4:7

Question: What are black holes?

Lane

Age 10

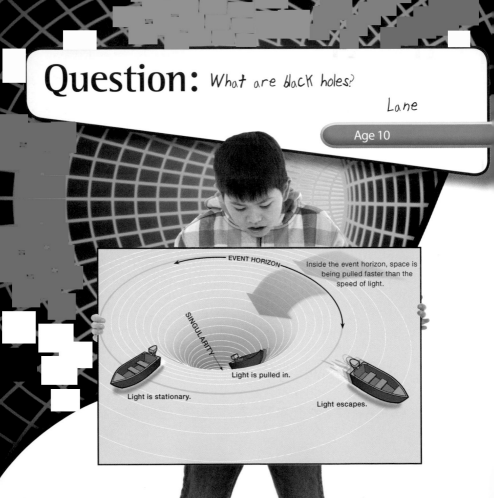

EVENT HORIZON

Inside the event horizon, space is being pulled faster than the speed of light.

SINGULARITY

Light is pulled in.

Light is stationary.

Light escapes.

Answer:

For by Him all things were created that are in heaven and that are on earth, visible and invisible, whether thrones or dominions or principalities or powers. All things were created through Him and for Him (Colossians 1:16).

Black holes are real objects that God made in space. Because they have so much mass, their gravity is so strong that light can't even escape from them. If light cannot escape a black hole, then it can never get to your eyes, so it appears black. When you close your eyes in a dark room, you can't see anything, and it appears black because light doesn't make it to your eye.

A black hole's gravity is so strong that it pulls light back into it. Imagine throwing a ball up into the sky — it would fall back down again, right?

In a black hole, it is actually doing more than just pulling *light* in. It is actually pulling *space itself* in faster than the speed of light. So light that is trying to travel away from a black hole moving at the speed of light gets sucked into it.

In a black hole, there is a certain distance away from it where the trend reverses and light is faster and can escape. That distance is called the "event horizon." But a black hole actually distorts the space around itself. Researchers recently found what they think is the largest black hole ever discovered. It's at the core of the galaxy called "NGC 1277."

Colossians 1:6; Nehemiah 9:6;
Revelation 21:1

13

Question:
Is it possible that there are living things in space?

Becca

Age 9

Answer:

For thus says the LORD, Who created the heavens, Who is God, Who formed the earth and made it, Who has established it, Who did not create it in vain, Who formed it to be inhabited: "I am the LORD, and there is no other (Isaiah 45:18).

Yes — there are people living on the space station right now. But they came from earth! The Bible seems to rule out any native intelligent life in outer space since they would be under the Curse with no possibility of salvation (Romans 8). Only the descendants of Adam can be saved (1 Corinthians 15:22–45). Earth was the center of life that God made in six days. God made the earth livable or habitable (Isaiah 45:18), and God never said other places in space were habitable. When Christ returns, it will be on the earth and nowhere else.

Of course, there are beings like angels, cherubim, and other heavenly host that are viewed as spiritual life in heaven. God *is* spirit (John 4:24), so it makes sense that He can make life in both physical and spiritual forms. We, as people, have a body *and* a spirit.

Spaceships, satellites, and probes have taken all sorts of bacteria to space when they didn't mean to. Surely some probes to places like Mars were not absent of bacteria. Many little microbes could also be whisked into space from our upper atmosphere. But keep in mind that these all originated on earth.

John 4:24; Isaiah 45:18

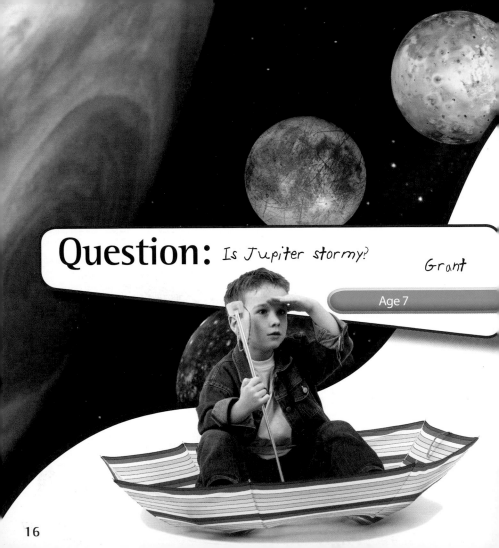

Question: Is Jupiter stormy?

Grant

Age 7

16

Answer:

Fire and hail, snow and clouds; stormy wind, fulfilling His word (Psalm 148:8).

Jupiter is the largest planet in our solar system. Unlike Mercury, Venus, Earth, and Mars, Jupiter is a giant gas planet, but deep inside it is likely made of rock and metallic gasses that have been compressed and solidified. The stripes that appear on the planet are actually generated by strong winds. Because of its gas composition and strong winds, it is prone to massive storms.

The biggest storm on Jupiter is called the Great Red Spot, and it appears as a large red spot on the planet. It's a storm that has been raging for a long time — it has been observed continuously since the 1800s. Imagine being stuck inside your house for an almost 200-year-long storm! We are not sure if God created Jupiter with the Great Red Spot storm, or if the storm started after God initially created everything. There would not be a problem in a perfect world before Adam and Eve sinned to have a storm like this on a planet that doesn't have life.

Jupiter is actually a rather hot planet. It gives off more heat energy than it receives. This is important because some people incorrectly think that Jupiter is billions of years old. If it were, it should have cooled off by now. But if it were created about 6,000 years ago, this explains why it still has heat to give off.

Job 26:12; Psalm 107:25

17

Question: What are comets and what are they made of?

Neva

Age 8

Answer:

Thus God made the firmament, and divided the waters which were under the firmament from the waters which were above the firmament; and it was so (Genesis 1:7).

Comets are icy objects in space that release dust or gas when they approach the sun. They are typically made of ice, dust, and frozen gases, and some even have a rocky core. Comets are very small compared to a planet and usually have highly elliptical (egg-shaped) orbits.

Some comets are called "sun-grazers." They completely disintegrate when they get close to the sun; they may even crash right into it! When a comet nears the sun, it heats up and the gases and ice break off of the comet, making it smaller and leaving a beautiful trail of debris. This is where meteor showers come from. When the earth passes through the previous path of a comet, these pieces burn up as they fall into our atmosphere. This means that comets can't last billions of years and this is a good confirmation that the solar system (including comets) is not that old.

The age of creation is based on the Bible's genealogies. When we calculate the numbers in these genealogies, we get an age around 6,000 years (e.g., 4,000 years from creation to Christ). Comets make sense in a young solar system.

Genesis 5:3–5

19

Question: How far away is the next galaxy?

Tallia

Age 9

20

Answer:

For as the heavens are higher than the earth, so are My ways higher than your ways, and My thoughts than your thoughts (Isaiah 55:9).

A galaxy is a system that usually consists of billions of stars held together by gravity. We see them far away and near our own galaxy. Our galaxy is called the Milky Way. The nearest galaxy depends on how we define a galaxy. There are masses of stars much smaller than the Milky Way that are considered a galaxy. There are many of these, and the close ones are also considered satellites of our own Milky Way galaxy. Think of all the moons, which are satellites that surround Jupiter. The smaller masses of stars are satellites to the Milky Way just like those moons are satellites of Jupiter.

If we count these satellites of the Milky Way as galaxies, then the next closest galaxy is Canis Major Dwarf, which is about 25,000 light years away. Of course, astronomers still debate about the specifics and classification of these minor galaxies, including this one. There are about 19 satellite galaxies in the next major galaxy, called Andromeda Galaxy (M31). But it would be the closest galaxy that is about the size of the Milky Way (2.5 million light years across). In fact, it is a little larger than the Milky Way, and it shares the same spiral shape. Spiral galaxies are good examples of why the universe is not billions of years old. If they were, the spiral arms should have all been wound up already!

Ecclesiastes 3:11; Job 22:12; Psalm 147:4

Question: How many planets are there? What is the smallest planet? Could planets hit each other?

Jackson, Gershom, & Annie

Ages 9, 8, & 10

22

Answer:

Can you bind the cluster of the Pleiades, or loose the belt of Orion?
(Job 38:31).

The definition of a planet was recently changed. Because of this change, the previous count of nine planets was changed to eight. Pluto is no longer considered a planet. According to the new definition, a planet must be massive enough to be nearly round, in orbit around the sun (usually in the same basic plane), and have control of its surroundings (e.g., moons, rings, and so on revolve around it.) By this definition, there are only eight planets (Mercury, Venus, Earth, Mars, Jupiter, Saturn, Uranus, and Neptune). Although Pluto used to be considered the smallest planet, the smallest one is now Mercury. Mercury is also the closest planet to the sun.

Planets have a fixed orbit at a certain distance around the sun, so none of them will ever collide. They are very far away from each other. There are things that collide with planets and moons, but these are smaller chunks of rock, like meteoroids. The orbits of some other items like comets *could* hit planets. They have an orbit that comes close to the sun and then travels far away from it. These could hit a planet, but it would still be a very rare event since the solar system is big and even planets are very small in this big system, but it does happen from time to time. For example, in 1994, Jupiter was hit by Comet Shoemaker-Levy 9.

Psalm 108:5; Psalm 57:11

HOLY
BIBLE

Question: Did Christians believe the earth was flat?

Kylie

Age 6

Answer:

It is He who sits above the circle of the earth, and its inhabitants are like grasshoppers, who stretches out the heavens like a curtain, and spreads them out like a tent to dwell in (Isaiah 40:22).

Most ancients believed in a round earth including Christians. Eratosthenes was an ancient geographer who even calculated the circumference of the earth about 200 B.C.! Very few Christians ever believed that the earth was flat. One Christian who did believe this was Lactantius (ca. A.D. 240–300). Sadly, he mixed the false flat-earth concept with his Christianity.

An overwhelming number of Christians opposed a flat earth, and for good reason. The Bible teaches against it in Isaiah 40:22 and Job 26:10. These verses point out that the earth is circular or round. Job even goes so far as to say that the earth hangs on nothing (Job 26:7)! This was confirmed when we sent satellites and people into space, and they could see and take pictures of the earth simply "hanging on nothing."

From the big picture though, Christians should always be careful about taking ideas that come from outside Scripture and mixing them with their Christianity. Instead, we should trust what God's Word says, since He knows best!

Isaiah 40:22; Job 26:7, 10

25

Question: Do meteors burn up and are they dangerous?

Simeon & Zachary

Ages 10 & 7

Answer:

Do not be overly wicked, nor be foolish: why should you die before your time? (Ecclesiastes 7:17).

Meteors are made from meteoroids and sometimes asteroids, which are bigger. Meteoroids are rocky and/or icy fragments (depending on comet remnants) that are smaller than asteroids and are found in many parts of space. Meteoroids, when they fall into earth's atmosphere, become "meteors." If some parts of a meteor don't burn up (due to the heated compression of the air in front of the meteor), those pieces are called "meteorites." Can they be dangerous? Yes, they can, but most are not. Most meteors typically burn up, with nothing left of them to fall out of the sky. It's actually rather enjoyable to watch as the meteors burn up — we often call the flashes of light across the night sky "falling stars" or "shooting stars," even though they are not really stars. But if the pieces are large and do not burn up all the way, then they can hit the ground really fast, sending a big shockwave! This can do serious damage.

A meteor that was about 50 feet in diameter (15 meters) hit the city of Chelyabinsk, Russia, on February 15, 2013. Much of the meteor burned up, but the rest of it shattered above the city and caused a lot of damage with the debris and shockwave. This rare event injured about 1,500 people.

Ecclesiastes 3:1; Romans 8:22

Question: How hot are the sun and other stars?

Eve

Age 8

Answer:

For no sooner has the sun risen with a burning heat than it withers the grass; its flower falls, and its beautiful appearance perishes. So the rich man also will fade away in his pursuits (James 1:11).

The sun is not too hot or too cold when compared to other stars. Typically, there is a range of temperatures for stars. Blue ones are much hotter, and red ones are much cooler. The surface temperature of the sun is about 10,000° Fahrenheit (or 5505° Celsius and 5778° Kelvin [K]).

The coolest stars (under 3500°K) are red. Next on the scale are red-to-orange stars, with a temperature of 3500–5000°K. Then there are yellow-to-white stars, which range from 5000–6000°K. This is where our sun would be, since it has an average surface temperature of 5778°K. Next are stars in the white-to-blue range, with temperatures of 6000°K — 7500°K.

Blue stars are the hottest (typically over 7500°K) and have three classes: A, B, and O. "A" contains temperatures above 7500°K, "B" contains temperatures over 11,000°K, and O contains temperatures over 25,000°K. The hotter the stars are, the more light they give off (known as luminosity).

Blue stars are a problem for those who believe in millions of years. Blue stars give off so much energy and burn their fuel so fast that they should not be able to last for long periods of time. But a recent creation of about 6,000 years helps to make sense of blue stars.

1 Corinthians 15:41

Question: What is the farthest that we've sent something into space?

Noah

Age 10

Answer:

And then He will send His angels, and gather together His elect from the four winds, from the farthest part of earth to the farthest part of heaven (Mark 13:27).

At this stage, we have sent something that has finally reached the outer edges of our solar system and is about to enter interstellar space. It is called the *Voyager 1* spacecraft. Launched in September of 1977 with the goal of studying the outer solar system, it routinely sends back data and pictures. This is easily the farthest that man has ever sent anything into space — and it is still working today! Interestingly, *Voyager 1* was supposed to study Jupiter, Saturn, and their associated moons, rings, and so on. When that was accomplished in November of 1980, the probe simply continued to travel to space. *Voyager 1* is not the only space probe that has been sent to the outer reaches of the solar system. In total, there have been four: *Voyager 1*, *Voyager 2*, *Pioneer 10*, and *Pioneer 11*. *Voyager 2* went to Jupiter, Saturn, Uranus, and Neptune. *Voyager 2* was the only spacecraft to visit Uranus and Neptune, and it is still going, though not as fast as *Voyager 1*.

Man has always been fascinated with finding out what is beyond, and yet so often we miss that the Creator Himself became a man (Jesus Christ) and came to seek us out. Let's not forget that.

Isaiah 55:9; Ephesians 4:10; Luke 19:10

Question:

What are the rings of planets made from?

Walton

Age 10

Answer:

For You are my rock and my fortress; therefore, for Your name's sake, lead me and guide me (Psalms 31:3).

Many planets have moons that orbit them. God has blessed the earth with one moon. But some planets even have beautiful rings that encircle them!

When we talk about planets with rings around them, Saturn is obviously the one many people think of. It is called the "Jewel of the Solar System." The rings are large and bright, so they are easy to see with a telescope. Galileo was the first to discover that Saturn had rings in 1610, though he was confused as to what they were. He was using very limited telescopes he had made.

But our solar system actually has four planets that have rings. Jupiter has rings (discovered in 1979), but they are very faint. Uranus has rings (discovered in 1977), as does Neptune (discovered in 1968 and 1984, but confirmed in 1989). Each ring orbits at a different speed, and each ring and gap or division between the rings are given names, too.

The rings are made up of dust, rock, and ice. Some of the particles are smaller than grains of sand but can be as large as a building.

Colossians 1:15–17

Question: What about the big bang?

Kylie

Age 6

Answer:

You alone are the LORD; You have made heaven, the heaven of heavens, with all their host, the earth and everything on it .... The host of heaven worships You (Nehemiah 9:6).

The supposed big bang is one of the popular atheistic models about the origin of the universe. It basically teaches that the universe created itself. There was nothing, then something popped into existence from nothing, rapidly "exploded," and is still expanding today. Actually, biblical creationists expect the heavens to be stretching out as well, but by the power of God, not by a big bang. There are big problems with the big-bang model. First, it conflicts with God's Word. The big-bang model has stars coming into existence before the earth, but God says the earth came before the stars. Also, according to the Bible, the age of the universe is about 6,000 years. This clearly disagrees with the billions of years required for the big bang.

The big bang has several scientific problems, too. Some well-meaning Christians have suggested that maybe God used the big bang, but if that were the case, then God really didn't do anything — and it contradicts His Word. The God of the Bible was intimately involved in creation from the very first verse of the Bible. The issue is whether we will trust a perfect God's Word when He speaks or imperfect human opinions about the past.

Isaiah 42:5, 44:24; Zechariah 12:1;
Colossians 2:8

Question:

How big is our galaxy?

Emma

Age 8

Answer:

But will God indeed dwell on the earth? Behold, heaven and the heaven of heavens cannot contain You. How much less this temple which I have built! (1 Kings 8:27).

Our galaxy is very big. A galaxy is not the universe, which is much bigger and contains all the galaxies. Our galaxy is called the Milky Way. It is about 12,000 light years across (1 light year = almost 5.878625 trillion miles). It is thought that 200 — 400 billion stars are within the Milky Way.

Compared to other galaxies, the Milky Way is actually a middle-sized one. There are some very large galaxies with stars estimated in the trillions.

There are smaller galaxies, too. Some are so small and near our own galaxy so they are considered satellites of the Milky Way. The stars used for constellations (like Orion, Bear, and Pleiades) are found within our own galaxy. Very few things can be seen with the naked eye outside of our galaxy, but there are a few things like the Andromeda Galaxy and Magellanic Clouds.

*Job 9:9; Job 38:31;
Amos 5:8*

37

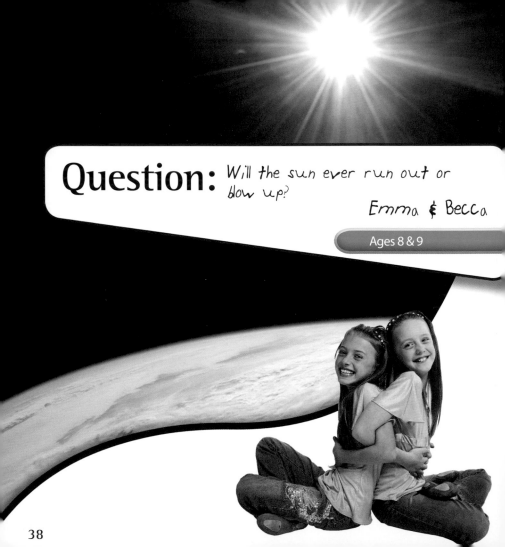

Question:
Will the sun ever run out or blow up?

Emma & Becca

Ages 8 & 9

38

Answer:

They shall fear You as long as the sun and moon endure, throughout all generations (Psalms 72:5).

God is an excellent designer! When He created all things, they were perfect (Genesis 1:31; Deuteronomy 32:4). There was no death, bloodshed, suffering . . . and no homework! The world really was perfect. But it wasn't just the world that was perfect — everything was, including the sun. It was perfectly designed by God. It has been consistently producing light and heat for earth since its creation on day 4 ("the greater light to rule the day"). There is no reason to assume that it will not continue to perform these duties until the end.

Keep in mind something that happened in the past that affects the whole of creation (Romans 8:20–22): the Curse. When Adam sinned against God, God cursed the ground and the animals and sentenced man to die (Genesis 3). The Curse affected everything (Romans 8:22). This would also affect the sun. This is why we will eventually need a new heavens and a new earth (Isaiah 66:17–22; 2 Peter 3:13; Revelation 21:1).

But until then, as long as the earth endures, God promised that day and night, cold and heat, seedtime and harvest, and winter and summer shall not cease (Genesis 8:22). So the sun, which is vital for this, will continue to do its created duties until the end.

Genesis 1:31, 8:22; Romans 8:22; 2 Peter 3:13

Question: What would happen if a comet ran into an asteroid?

Noah

Age 9

Answer:

For since the creation of the world His invisible attributes are clearly seen, being understood by the things that are made, even His eternal power and Godhead, so that they are without excuse (Romans 1:20).

Comets are made mostly of dust, rock, and ice, while asteroids are primarily made of rock. A snowball hitting a rock might be similar to what it would be like if a comet hit an asteroid at high speed. The frozen water on a comet vaporizes when the comet nears the sun and makes a comet tail that points away from the sun (called a "coma"). This would make it easier for a comet to break apart than an asteroid. So the comet, depending on the size, would likely be the one that broke up more.

Interestingly, NASA had a mission to smash into a comet. The comet, Tempel 1, was a city-sized comet that was discovered in 1867 by Ernst Tempel. It orbits the sun every 5.5 years. NASA decided to collide an object into it called an "impactor" the size of a small desk that weighed 820 pounds (370 kg.)! This impactor was monitored by a spacecraft called *Deep Impact* to get a glimpse of what was below the surface of the comet.

Many researchers on this mission were hoping to learn a little more about "an evolutionary history" instead of the true history in the Book of Genesis. God's creation is incredible to explore!

Genesis 1:14

Question: How old is space and the universe?

Trace

Age 6

Answer:

In the beginning God created the heavens and the earth (Genesis 1:1).

The "heavens and the earth" were created by God at the beginning, when He created time (Genesis 1:1) on day 1 of the creation week. There is no word for "universe" in Hebrew, which is the language of the Old Testament. But when "heavens" and "earth" are used together like this, it means the whole of creation, which includes the universe (and space).

God created the universe on day 1 and Adam on day 6. When we add up the genealogies in the Bible from Adam to Abraham in Genesis 5 and 11, it comes to about 2,000 years. Most people agree that Abraham lived about 2,000 B.C., which is approximately 4,000 years ago from today. So we know the universe is around 6,000 years old.

Some try to say the age of the universe is 13–15 billion years! This date comes from people who make assumptions about the past and ignore the Bible's account of creation. You can either trust an all-knowing, perfect God about His creation, or you can trust imperfect people's guesses about the past. God is always right, and if people ever disagree with God's Word, then they are the ones who are wrong. God and His Word are trustworthy and true from the very first verse.

Genesis 1:1; Isaiah 42:5;
Hebrews 11:3

HOLY BIBLE

43

Yearly Meteor Shower Dates

Name	Approximate Date Range	Likely Peak
Quadrantids	January 2–3	January 3
Lyrids	April 20–22	April 22
Eta Aquarids	May 4–6	May 6
Delta Aquarids	July 29–30	July 29
Perseids	August 10–13	August 12
Draconids	October 7–10	October 8
Orionids	October 18–23	October 22
Leonids	November 16–18	November 18
Taurids	November 8–10	November 18
Geminids	December 10–12	December 14

Table of Planets and the first 5 *Dwarf Planets*

		Planet or Dwarf Planet	Average distance from the sun (in millions of miles)	Moons	Average Length of year in earth days/years
	Mercury	Planet	36	0	88 days
	Venus	Planet	67	0	224.7 days
	Earth	Planet	93	1	1 year
	Mars	Planet	142	2	687 days
	Jupiter	Planet	484	67	11.9 years
	Saturn	Planet	888	62	27.9 years
	Uranus	Planet	1,784	27	84.3 years
	Neptune	Planet	2,799	13	164.8 years
	Pluto	Dwarf Planet	3,670	5	248 years
	Eris	Dwarf Planet	10,180	1	557 years
	Haumea	Dwarf Planet	6,432	2	282 years
	Makemake	Dwarf Planet	4,214	0	310 years
	Ceres	Dwarf Planet	413	0	4.6 years

Definitions

asteroids: Rocky bodies too small to be planets, usually with an irregular shape. There is a large asteroid belt that orbits the sun between Mars and Jupiter. Many asteroids are found throughout our solar system.

meteoroids: Rocky fragments even smaller than asteroids, found in many parts of space. Many are even intermingled in the asteroid belt. When meteoroids fall into earth's atmosphere, they become meteors. If some parts o don't burn up, those pieces are called meteorites.

comets: Objects made mostly of ice, frozen gas, dust, and rock that make lo elliptical orbits around the sun. A comet usually leaves a debris tail a approaches the sun and heats up. The tail of a comet always stretch away from the sun.

planets: Must be massive enough to be nearly round, in orbit around the s (usually in the same basic plane), and have control of its surroundir (e.g., moons, rings, and so on revolve around it). By this current definiti there are only eight planets (Mercury, Venus, Earth, Mars, Jupiter, Satu Uranus, and Neptune).

dwarf planets: Dwarf planets do not fulfill all the requirements of a planet but significantly larger than asteroids. Two dwarf planets were at c time classed as planets: Ceres and Pluto.

axies: Systems of billions of stars held together by gravity. Our solar system is in the Milky Way galaxy, which is a spiral galaxy. Many galaxies that are not spiral have shapes like elliptical, round, toothpick, and ring shapes, among many others.

bulas: Large cloud-like structures (interstellar) made of dust and gases that give off light in beautiful arrays and shapes. They can be many light-years across.

asar: Quasar stands for "quasi-stellar radio source." They are among the most distant and brightest (luminous) objects we know of. They emit immense amounts of energy as well. There is still much to learn about quasars.

t-year: A measure of distance, not time. One light-year is how far light can travel in one year. This is roughly 5,878,625,000,000 miles or 9,460,730,000,000 km.

Answers Are Always Important!

The Bible is truly filled some amazing answers for some of our toughest faith questions. The Answers Book for Kids series answers questions from children around the world in this multi-volume series. Each volume will answer over 20 questions in a friendly and readable style appropriate for children 6–12 years old; and each covers a unique topic including, Creation and the Fall; Dinosaurs and the Flood of Noah; God and the Bible; and Sin, Salvation, and the Christian Life, and more!